Mortgage Modifications Made Easy!

How to Reduce Your Home Payment in Ten Minutes
or Less!

By Bob Boog
Author of *Selling Homes 1-2-3*

Mortgage Modifications Made Easy: How to reduce your home payment in ten minutes or less!

copyright 2010 by Robert Boog

ths international publishing.
23916 Lyons Avenue
Newhall, Ca. 91321

Some pictures from istock.com

ISBN: 978-0-9666130-9-4

Table of Contents

Legal Disclaimer Stuff

Just so you know, copyright law says that you may not distribute this book in any form, in any medium, without prior written permission from Bob Boog, ths international publishing or Bob Boog Realty, Inc.

No income, actual time savings or financial claims are made or inferred in this work.

The contents of this book are my opinions and observations, based on my own experience and should not be taken as anything more than that.

Nothing in this product should be construed as legal or other professional advice.

If you need legal advice, seek the assistance of an appropriate licensed professional in the relevant field.

Some of the things discussed in this book involve activities which are regulated in various jurisdictions. You are responsible for complying with the laws where you live and where you conduct business.

You are solely responsible for the consequences of your use of this material.

My goal is to help you improve your odds for getting a loan modification approved, but there is NO guarantee that providing this information alone will do it.

Ultimately it will be up to you (and your lender) to do so.

Why Do a Mortgage Modification?

Many homeowners wonder if filing a mortgage modification is worth the time and effort. Some experts say that it takes too long and is too much work. If you are in foreclosure, they say, walking away from a home or doing a short sale is a better option. Well, I'm here to say that doing a loan modification should be your ***first option*** because it takes about 10 minutes to do, it doesn't cost a dime upfront and it solves a major problem for most homeowners. It's like giving a housewife an aspirin when she has a throbbing headache. It makes things better for everybody in the house!

In addition, there are more benefits. If a homeowner's loan modification is denied under HAMP - (Home Affordable Modification Program) and if the owner then agrees to do a short sale, the Federal government will offer the homeowners **$3,000** for moving expenses. But if a homeowner does the short sale first (without attempting to modify via Hamp) the owner *won't* get the $3,000. In addition, some bankruptcy lawyers claim that a bankruptcy judge may ask an owner if he had tried to do a loan modification before approving the terms of the bankruptcy. So even if you do the loan modification yourself, and even if you don't think you will qualify, you are better off trying to do a loan modification. This guide will attempt to improve your odds for getting it approved too.

How Do I Know if I Qualify?

Not everyone qualifies for a mortgage modification. To see if you qualify for the most popular mortgage modification, the federal government's HAMP program (Home Affordable Mortgage Program) take this quick and easy test. If you can answer "yes" to these three questions, you'll probably qualify.

1. **Is the house with the mortgage you wish to modify your principal residence?**
(You claim it on your taxes as your principal residence.)

2. **Are you about to be one payment behind on your mortgage (but not more than 12 payments) and is your loan balance LESS than $729,750?**

3. **Is your house payment MORE than 31% of your gross income?**
Not sure? **Let's do the math.**
Let's suppose John makes $3,850 per month before deductions.
 3850 x 31%=$1,193.

If John's house payment is **LESS than** $1,193, John would answer "NO" and would NOT qualify.
But if John's payment is MORE **than $1,193**, then John would answer "Yes".

If you answered "yes" to all three questions, then you **probably** qualify! (There may be other guidelines that might exclude a homeowner (see the next page), but these are the general ones to follow). You have until **December 31, 2012** to get busy! That's the deadline.

What Might Disqualify Me?

Prior to getting your Hamp loan modification approved, you will need to sign and date the **Dodd Frank Certification Form**. This form states that you are not guilty of tax evasion, felony larceny, theft, forgery or money laundering.

Servicer: _____   Loan Number _____ ←

HELP FOR AMERICA'S HOMEOWNERS.

MAKING HOME AFFORDABLE

Dodd-Frank Certification

The following information is requested by the federal government in accordance with the Dodd-Frank Wall Street Reform and Consumer Protection Act (Pub. L. 111-203). **You are required to furnish this information.** The law provides that no person shall be eligible to receive assistance from the Making Home Affordable Program, authorized under the Emergency Economic Stabilization Act of 2008 (12 U.S.C. 5201 *et seq.*), or any other mortgage assistance program authorized or funded by that Act, if such person, in connection with a mortgage or real estate transaction, has been convicted, within the last 10 years, of any one of the following: (A) felony larceny, theft, fraud or forgery, (B) money laundering or (C) tax evasion.

Borrower	**Co-Borrower**
☐ I have not been convicted within the last 10 years of any one of the following in connection with a mortgage or real estate transaction: (a) felony larceny, theft, fraud or forgery, (b) money laundering or (c) tax evasion	☐ I have not been convicted within the last 10 years of any one of the following in connection with a mortgage or real estate transaction: (a) felony larceny, theft, fraud or forgery, (b) money laundering or (c) tax evasion

In making this certification, I/we certify under penalty of perjury that all of the information in this document is truthful and that I/we understand that the Servicer, the U.S. Department of the Treasury, or their agents may investigate the accuracy of my statements by performing routine background checks, including automated searches of federal, state and county databases, to confirm that I/we have not been convicted of such crimes. I/we also understand that knowingly submitting false information may violate Federal law.

→ _____   Date: ____/____/____

→ _____   Date: ____/____/____

OK, Who Died and Made Me King?

Right now you may be wondering, okay so who died and made me the mortgage modification king? Very quickly: My name is Bob Boog and I am a real estate broker and owner of Bob Boog Realty in Newhall, Ca. I have worked full-time in real estate since 1978 and am the author of three books on real estate. I have watched the industry fly through several roller coaster cycles which has brought us to this present moment. I've done my own loan modification and my wife and I have helped several other people do loan modifications too.

This information is provided at a low charge. Don't let the low price fool you. The little gems sprinkled throughout it can have a profound impact on your success.

Some of what you're about to read in this book may seem obvious to you. Some of it you may disagree with, or you might mentally say, "HA! That won't work".

My goal with this book is to help you **improve your odds** so that you can modify your loan by yourself quickly and easily. I want you to develop a mindset that will, hopefully, enable you to get there more quickly and certainly, with fewer missteps than you might otherwise encounter. I want to help fill in **a gap of information** that I think exists in this field.

Why Do Banks Modify Loans?

President Obama has declared that this is a historical time of economic crisis. Because of the dire situation and fear of that the world economy is heading into a depression, lenders are hoping to head off the crisis by modifying home loans. Most lenders have too many foreclosures on their books and would rather take less each month and have someone living in the property rather than foreclose and have the property be vacant. After all, foreclosures are time-consuming, expensive and problematic. A foreclosure often takes 12 months of man-hours to finalize and vandalism is common.

In addition, the prices of homes might decline further. So by the time the Lender finally puts the house up for sale, the Lender might lose even more money. Even the cleanest family home can quickly turn into the neighborhood eyesore.

Modifying means to lower the interest rate, reduce the loan balance or create more affordable loans that will help to save the economy as well as help save the owner's credit. Mortgage modifications also help entire communities survive a deteriorating economy. Homeowners can keep their property as well as make tax payments to Federal, state and local governments. Is there a maximum loan amount for loan modifications? Yes. The amount you owe can't be more than **$729,750 on a one-unit single family residence and $934,200 for 2 units.**

What is the main reason that lenders modify loans?

To keep the money rolling in without problems. See, just because President Obama wants banks to modify loans **doesn't** mean that the lender is going to forgive your **entire** debt. Some people actually expect that to happen – they'll want the lender to reduce a $160,000 loan balance to like... $9,000. Or they assume their payment will go from $5,000 a month to $50 a month, but that's not going to happen.

As Joan Rivers would say, "Can we talk?"

Your Lender's Job

A comic once joked that a lender's job is to open envelopes filled with money each month keep part of it for himself and send the rest to his investor. It's partially true! Your lender very much wants to continue receiving little envelopes filled with money from you each and every month. He's NOT drunk or stupid. The lender will probably be okay with receiving **about 30% less,** but not 90% less each month, do you catch my drift?

Old payment: $1,000 x 30% = $300.   New payment: $600.

Debt Forgiveness

We are going to be talking about principal debt forgiveness later on in this book. I been involved in cases where lenders have forgiven part or all of **a second** mortgage for an owner but we're mainly going to be talking about only modifying your **First loan** here, so here goes.

In most First Loan cases, lenders will waive late fees, extend the loan term and lower interest rates to as low as 2% (to achieve a loan modification). Usually the late fees and unpaid interest payments get added back to the loan. The net effect is a lower payment to assist the homeowner, but no debt forgiven. But don't get discouraged, we'll talk more about debt forgiveness in a bit.

What's Involved in a Loan Modification?

Though a mortgage modification may sound complicated, it's not. It just requires completing some simple financial forms. It's almost like qualifying for a home loan in reverse. Filling out the basic RMA request (see pages 71-73) collecting the necessary documents and sending them to your lender takes about ten minutes. That's the first part.

The second part of a loan modification involves **WAITING for the lender** to finalize things. Warning: sometimes banks lose applications, financials, things you've faxed to them ten times. Sometimes they fail to call back after you call them and leave messages. Whatever. During the waiting time, you will need to make several trial payments before getting your approved documents. Be forewarned: **Getting your modification can take anywhere from 30 days or several months!** Keep repeating this mantra: having my house payment reduced is worth it! The third and last part involves signing your modification agreement. YAY!

How do I start?

The first step involves figuring out if your loan qualifies for the Home Affordable Modification Program. To qualify, your loan must be owned by Freddie Mac or Fannie Mae (two companies who buy and sell people's mortgages.) You can find out by visiting the Making Homes Affordable website. Have your loan number handy. Click the "Loan Lookup" Tab and then enter your loan number.

 If the link doesn't work, type this url into your browser:

http://www.makinghomesaffordable.gov/

Or if you are not computer-savvy, pick up the phone and call your lender. Most have automated call centers. They will require you to input your loan number and last four digits of your social security number, so have them ready.

Question: What if my loan is NOT owned by Freddie Mac or Fannie Mae?

Answer: If your loan does not show up on the Making Homes Affordable **website, you should still continue to read on. You will need to negotiate directly with your bank. The process may not be as quick and easy, but most banks will still modify the terms for you – even if they say they won't!**

A General Overview of the Process

Okay, according to the website, yes, my loan is owned by Fannie Mae. So I now contact my lender. Let's suppose my lender is Bank of America. I will call and ask for the Loss Mitigation Department. I would like to get a Making **Homes Affordable Modification Request Form**. (See pages 71-73). This is the form I am asking about. Bank of America will either send me the form or tell me to go to the Making Homes Affordable website to download one. Here is a general overview of what to expect:

1. I'll fill out the HAMP request form (pgs 71-73) and sign it. The form tells me what financial documents I will need to send to Bank of America. So I send the documentation and application - either by fax or mail to Bank of America.

Note: when I fill out this application and send my financial documentation to Bank of America, I will be applying for the **Hardship *Affidavit*.**

2. Next, Bank of America may call me to see that I received their package, **so I will want to take BofA's phone calls and not ignore them.** I might receive a letter notifying me that I have been accepted and that the bank wants me to make three trial payments, so I make sure that Bank of America receives these payments on the first day of each new month.

So I make my payment each month via the telephone and write down the tracking number that they give me.

3. Next, I will receive the HAMP Affidavit. I will fill it out and return it to Bank of America with the **updated** financial data that they requested - meaning I'll send them more recent paystubs, bank statements and/or a profit and loss statement.

4. Important, the trial period of my lower payments may stretch out longer – **from three payments** to about **seven trial** payments before I finally receive my final modification agreement from Bank of America.

Again, I make sure that each payment is received by Bank of America by the first of each new month by wiring the money or just calling. I'll write down the tracking number!

5. I will receive the FINAL loan mod agreement, so I will want to call Bank of America to let them know, as they may make arrangements for a free notary service for me!

What if the loan is NOT owned by Freddie or Fannie?

If your bank is an **FHA loan**, the government offers a special program for FHA loans. For all other loans, call your lender and ask for their **Loss Mitigation Dept**. Request that a loan modification package be mailed to you. Ask the specialist for their name, and write it down in a notebook or journal. Eventually you will have a "negotiator" assigned to your file, and you'll want to get that person's direct phone number and email address too.

Along with completing a modification request form similar to the one on pages 71-73, my lender, Wells Fargo, wanted the usual financial stuff from me, such as:

1. Enough paystubs to complete a one month period or if I am self-employed a Year-to-Date Profit & Loss Statement. Or a letter from Social Security to verify my Social

Security or Disability income. Written proof of child support. [Note: whatever kind of monthly or annual income must have written verification.]

2. The prior year's W-2's, or Federal Income taxes or a letter explaining why I don't file taxes.
3. Three bank statements.
4. An explanation for why I need the loan modification.
5. A utility bill to prove that I currently reside at the property.
6. Proof of insurance (Declaration Page) to show that my insurance is current.
7. Proof of property taxes and that my taxes are current.
8. Proof that my HOA - home owner association fees have been paid (if applicable)
9. A signed 4506 tax form that allows Wells Fargo to check my income with what I had sent to the IRS.
10. Next, Wells Fargo may call me to see that I have received their package, so I will want to take their phone calls and not ignore them.
11. I might receive a letter notifying me that I have been accepted and that the bank wants me to make a few trial payments, so I make sure that Wells Fargo receives these payments on the first day of each new month.
12. The trial period of my lower payments may stretch out longer before I finally receive my final modification agreement from Wells Fargo. Somebody from Wells Fargo may call me to make sure that I received my loan mod agreement, so I will want to call them back, as they may make arrangements for a free notary service for me.

Note: even if my loan does not show up on the Making Homes Affordable website, the two methods of loan modifications are very similar!

Gathering Income Information

As you can tell by reading the general overviews, your lender will only count income that **can be verified**. It is not sufficient to say that you make $500 per month by recycling bottles. Or that you receive $800 in child support from your ex-spouse. Expect that a lender will want you to see written proof. Lenders will want you to document your income via letters, tax returns, court transcripts, bank statements, rental receipts, etc. This begs the question: "What if I receive part of my income in cash?" and/or "What if I am self employed?" How can I best document my income?

Read on!

What to Do if You are Self-Employed

If you are self-employed you will need to send your last year's Federal tax returns, plus send a current year's Profit and Loss Statement. I provided a sample Profit and Loss Statement [page 50] and an Excel P&L form is included in forms package at www.short-sales1-2-3.com/loanmodforms.html. The reason you might want to have a Profit and Loss Statement in Excel format is so that you can modify it. Because the lender may ask you for a 3 month P&L, or a 6 month P&L or a statement that covers an entire year.

What if I Own Two Businesses?

If you are self-employed and own two businesses, you will need to send a copy of last year's Federal tax returns. You will also want to include a current year's Profit and Loss Statement – one for each business. Or, one P&L statement that mentions both businesses. Either way is acceptable.

What if I Don't Have Microsoft Excel?

You can download a FREE Spreadsheet program that works just as well as Microsoft Excel at www.openoffice.org. Then fill in one of the P&L statements that you have downloaded at www.short-sales1-2-3.com/loanmodforms.html. (There's a video that shows you how to modify a spreadsheet if you are not familiar with it.) But if you already know how to work a spreadsheet? Great. Just fuggetabout it! You're ahead of the game.

What Does the HAMP Request Affidavit Look Like?

✓ As a bonus of this book, you will find the 3 page RMA form on pages 70-73. This is the HAMP request for a loan modification form that you need to fill out to get started.

What are Some Common Mistakes People Make?

Many homeowners have reservations about filling out the HAMP request form by themselves. Why? They are afraid of making a mistake. Having helped about 50 homeowners fill out applications, here are the most common mistakes.

1. **Address on RMA form does not match address on paystubs or tax returns.** This by far is the number one mistake. If your address does not match, you had better explain why. Remember, the HAMP program is NOT for people with rentals. If your address doesn't match, they'll probably think you own a rental and don't occupy the property.

2. **Failure to file tax returns**. If you haven't filed, go to see a local tax person and get your taxes done...even if you owe.

3. **Name on RMA form does not match name on loan**. If you are married, both parties will need to submit their financial information. Or if Aunt Susan co-signed with you for the loan, she is most likely going to have to bring in her financial stuff too – not just you.

4. **Failure to include a utility bill or proof of residency.** Again, the HAMP program is for owner-occupants, not landlords. You must provide proof that you are living at the property address.

A popular question people ask is: "What will my new interest rate be? Or, "How long does this process take?" And the truthful answer is: "I don't know".

The interest rate given by the HAMP program is usually a pretty good one and how long the process takes depends upon their caseload.

Have You Already been Declined by Your Lender?

If you have applied for a loan modification (but NOT through the HAMP program) and were declined, read through this book completely and then reapply through HAMP. First try to find out **why your loan mod was declined**. Your lender will usually let you try again through the Hamp program if you give them a good reason (example: "I forgot to include some additional income that I regularly receive").

If you have applied through HAMP and have been declined, you still may have options through the HAFA program (such as doing a short sale and receiving $3,000 in moving expenses) or bankruptcy. **If you have questions about this, contact an attorney**.

The biggest thing that will screw things up is failing *to make your monthly payments **on time*** during the trial period. Under the Making Home Affordable Program, the homeowner will be given payments under a trial period. These trial payments MUST always be received on time -- or the loan mod may be rejected completely, or you may have to restart the entire process! So make your payment *via the telephone* or **wire the funds**. Either way, write down **the tracking number** given to you by the bank.

What Else Do I Need to Get Started?

Some basic things you'll need to get started:

1. Patience – expect to be put on hold with the lender.
2. Computer with Internet connection
3. Telephone
4. Fax
5. Notebook – to take notes
6. Calculator
7. Copier (or access to one)
8. Ability to press buttons to navigate the lender's phone system
9. Lots of Patience – umm, did I mention this already? Let's continue.

Six Strategies for Success!

Six Strategies to Help Improve Your Odds of Approval

Because there may be many different people reading this book, I am including other strategies that may not be relevant to you but are sometimes critical. So read on, with the idea that some of these tactics may be helpful to you, while others may not apply.

Strategy #1: First Diagnose the Problem

Many people go to a doctor because they are in pain, but they don't know exactly what the problem is. For example, a patient might say, "My side aches." To diagnose what ails the patient, the doctor will ask a series of questions, starting with "Where exactly does it hurt?"

Similarly, when people call me to ask if I can help them modify their loan, I'll need to diagnose the problem to see if a mortgage modification will actually work for the homeowner. (And see if they can even qualify.) I'll need to ask the right questions and carefully listen to my customer to see what the problem is.

For example, a homeowner may call and say "Can you make my payments lower?" Many loan mod specialists will immediately answer, "Yes, yes of course we can. We can make them at least $600 per month lower" without asking the caller another question.

And maybe it's true –that the specialist can save the owner $600 a month.

But there are other things you have to consider too. Such as:

"Are you interested in staying in your home?"

"Are you employed or do you receive Social Security income?"

"Are you self-employed?"

"Did you file taxes last year? If so, how much income did you declare?"

 Important: a successful mortgage modification is based on the assumption that a homeowner *still wishes to stay in the home.*

Anything else will be a different solution.

The owner must have a burning desire to stay in the property. If the owner wants to stay but has waited too long, there might be a problem too. If the owner says, "***The trustee sale date is set for next week.***" Then your answer might be, "Hmm, have you talked with a lawyer about filing for bankruptcy?"

I mention this because many people have heard that once you file a HAMP Affidavit and the lender receives it, the lender must automatically give a 45 day stay of foreclosure. Meaning that the lender won't foreclose for about a month and a half. That's not totally true. Here's why.

Let's suppose that I have Mrs. Jones' financial papers and I fax them to her lender. Her bank might take up to three days to "image" those papers. So if I sent them on a Tuesday, and called the bank on Wednesday to see if they had received them, 99% of the time, the bank will say "No." What? It's true. The bank will usually tell you that it takes a few days for them to "image" them so that the documents can be seen on their computer screens. Okay, so let's say that it's now Friday, I call the lender and ask, "Have you received my papers?" Now the bank says, "Yes, but we had to send them to our investor, and it will take a few days for the investor to image the files."

"Your investor? Who is your investor?"

"Our investor is Fannie Mae. And Fannie Mae takes at least four days to image their uploaded files."

I guess what I'm saying, is that beware of cutting things too close to the wire. Often people in foreclosure are procrastinators who wait till the last minute, then want someone else to pull a rabbit out of the hat and save their homes. Unfortunately, Houdini has passed away. Likewise, you won't be able to save all of them.

This is an important concept. You will not be successful on every loan modification.

You have probably heard the saying, "Where there's a will, there's a way," right? I think it rings true almost every time. So if someone is motivated, they will be calling the bank too to stay on top and do whatever it takes to get the job done. But it's very difficult to help an owner who is NOT motivated to stay in his home!

Question: What if the homeowner says "No, I'm not interested in staying in this house. **I lost my job and hate living here. Or I'd love to let it go into foreclosure and in a couple of years try and buy something else.**"

What then? The answer to this question can be found in strategy number two!

So keep reading!

A Simple Idea that Saved a Homeowner from Losing Her Home.

✓ **Purchase a spiral notebook** and keep this journal by your telephone or computer. Jot down your loan number and the bank's phone number for handy reference and then whenever you call the lender, notate the date, time, and the name of the person you spoke with. Scribble brief notes of **what was said during your conversations** too.

MY LIFE BROKEN DOWN INTO SEGMENTS

WORKING

SLEEPING

EATING

LOOKING FOR THINGS
I HAD JUST A
MINUTE AGO

You may forget a small detail, but your lender won't. Why? Because your lender will record ALL of your phone conversations with them. This little tip may come in handy if and when you need to remind someone of something that was promised to you earlier. Because you can then point out a specific date and the bank can review their tapes!

In this example, the homeowner reminded the bank person of her conversation. A week later, the bank foreclosed! But because she documented her conversations, **the sale was RESCINDED by the bank,** and she and her husband didn't lose title to their home. Guess what saved her? Her spiral notebook and the little notes that she had jotted down—it gave the bank the right date and time to check their recorded conversations.

Strategy #2: Differentiate the Situation

I'm going to switch hats for a minute and talk about what most lenders look for in order to approve a client for a mortgage modification.

1. The homeowner had made their payments regularly but is now experiencing a hardship or situation that has reduced his/her income and may affect the ability to make timely monthly payments.

2. The homeowner's mortgage payment alone is more than 31% of his gross monthly income.

3. The homeowner has a high fixed rate or an adjustable rate loan that's going to be recast to a much higher rate very soon.

4. The homeowner occupies the property as his **primary residence** and wishes to continue doing so.

5. The homeowner is NOT currently in bankruptcy nor is he more than 12 months in arrears.

As you look at things from the lender's point of view, you may realize that **not every homeowner who wishes to modify his mortgage will qualify!**

• A homeowner who purchased a home with a low fixed rate loan for ten years, for example, might NOT be able to get his rate adjusted down further. (It doesn't hurt to try, but don't hold your breath).

• A homeowner who purchased with a slightly higher interest rate a year ago and is now hoping to reduce the principal balance of his loan.

• An owner who receives **cash** payments and cannot document his income may not qualify. Should she still apply? Absolutely! She can send the bank a Profit and Loss Statement, can't she?

What if you are a homeowner who has been turned down by your lender for a HAMP loan modification? Answer: don't just walk away. Call your lender and ask about **the HAFA program. You may be eligible to receive $3,000 in moving expenses**.

What does **HAFA** stand for? The Home Affordable Foreclosure Alternatives Program

To qualify for HAFA, the property MUST be your principal residence - investors are not accepted in this part of the program

•2.   Your loan MUST be older than January 1, 2009 - any loan after this date - don't count

•3.   You MUST be delinquent or AT RISK - bank will determine "at risk'

•4.   Your principal balance MUST be less than $729,750

•5.   Your income MUST be 31% more than your mortgage payment

Another **MUST**... you MUST have gone to your mortgage servicer/bank and have requested a loan modification and one of the following has happened:

- accepted,
- accepted and fail,
- **denied**, or
- can't afford the loan modification - so you turn it down

Another note: Your servicer/bank MUST offer you the HAFA if you meet the above. The servicer has 30 days in order to offer you the HAFA program after you meet one of the above and after doing the short sale, you should be eligible for the $3,000 in moving expenses.

Can I Modify my Rental Property Loan?
What about an investor who owns a rental property? Will a lender modify his loan? Maybe yes and maybe no. Should the owner still try to modify it? Yes. Absolutely! But if so, the landlord should disclose this information to a tenant. Otherwise, when some person comes to appraise the property, the tenant might fear that they might never get their security deposit back. See the sample disclosure found on the next page.

LANDLORD PROPERTY DISCLOSURE

Date: _____

This agreement is between _____ ("Landlord") and
_____("Tenant") regarding the
rental property at _____ ("The Property"). Landlord
makes the following disclosure with regard to the Property:

1. Tenant acknowledges and agrees that Landlord is currently involved in a loan modification on the property which may or may not be approved by landlord's lender(s). **Landlord may be behind on his payments**.
2. Tenant is aware that if the loan modification is declined, landlord may elect to do a short-sale on the property which may affect tenant's use and quiet enjoyment of the property. Tenant agrees to cooperate with said short-sale.
3. In any case, whether landlord is successful or not at modifying the loan or doing a short-sale, the tenant shall continue to make timely monthly payments to landlord.
4. Tenant's security deposit of ($_____) shall be promptly refunded (within two (2) days) if the tenant is asked to leave the premises due to a short sale of the property **or foreclosure**.

Understood and agreed to on this _____ day of _____20____ .

_____
Tenant   Landlord
State of _____
County of _____

On _____ before me, _____notary
public

personally appeared _____who
proved to me on the basis of satisfactory evidence to be the person(s) whose name(s) is/are subscribed to the within instrument and acknowledged to me that he/she/they executed the same in his/her/their authorized capacity(ies), and that by his/her/their signature(s) on the instrument the person(s) acted, executed the instrument. WITNESS my hand and official seal.

Signature _____

Before Jumping to Reapply to the Hamp Program

If someone previously didn't qualify for the bank's typical loan modification but didn't use the Hamp Program, he should try to find out if there was a problem and proactively try to solve it first. For example, if low income was an issue before, maybe he/she can:

- Trade in a car and buy a cheaper one
- Ask relatives for money to bring a loan current or pay off credit cards
- Find a contributor to help out with payments (**not a co-signor**- we'll talk about this strategy shortly)
- Rent out bedrooms to college students/lodgers

All of these things are available and most will help you to qualify for your Hamp loan modification. Some owners will also contact a lawyer. That's often a good idea too. Be aware that most lenders are willing to explain things if you ask. For example, you may have been denied because of "insufficient income". Call up your lender to see how much would be sufficient. Or, perhaps you moved out of your home and you were declined. But what if you moved out in order to comfort your aging mother? So you would like to keep your present house and rent it out, and perhaps move back to it later? Will a lender modify your loan if you find yourself in this situation? Some lenders will.

Strategy #3: Carefully Review Documents for Errors!

If you are doing your own modification, it's important to follow directions. Your lender is going to ask you to provide copies of simple documentation such as W-2s, paystubs and bank statements. Remember, you only need to send **your Federal tax return**, **not your State return.**

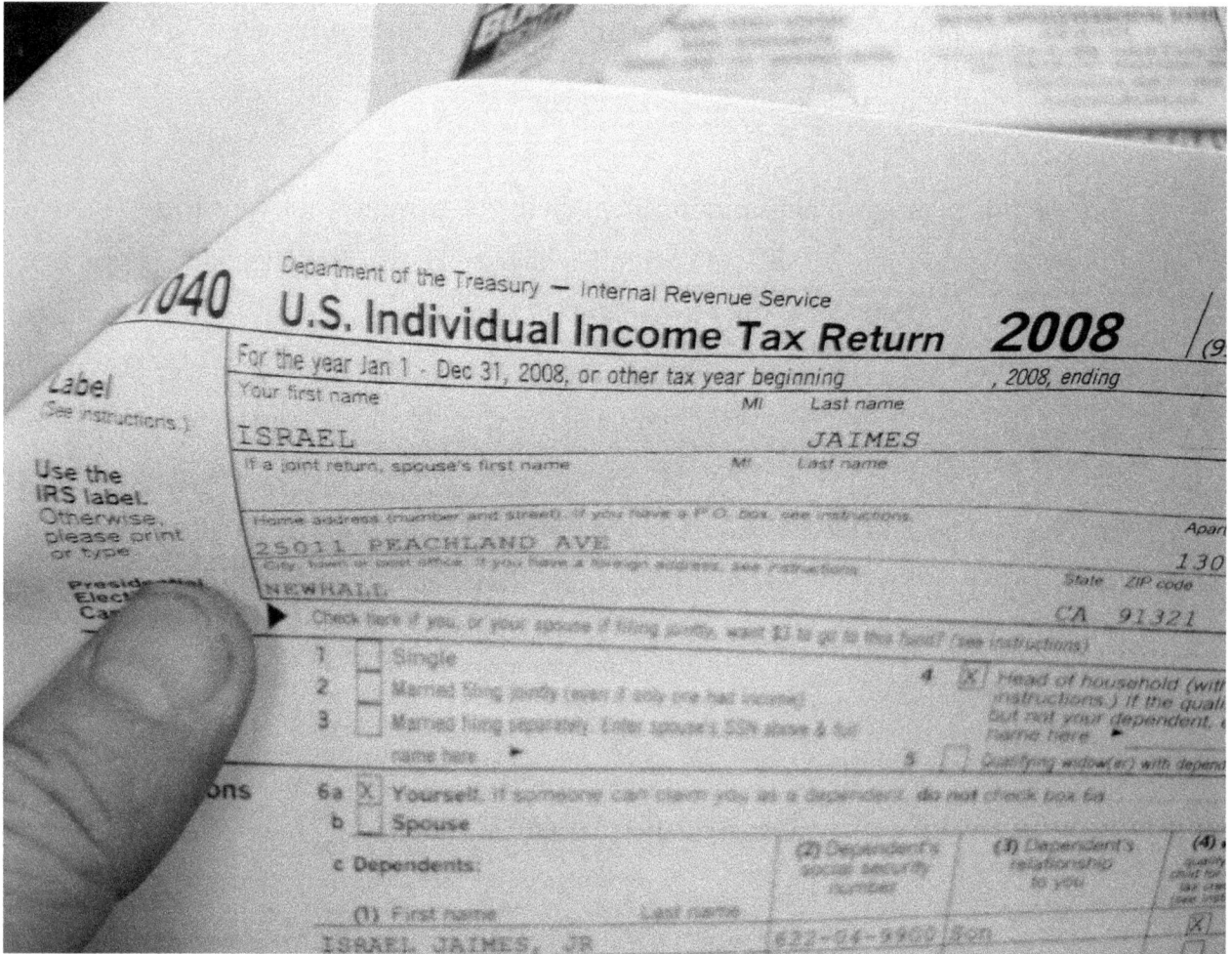

Also, **send copies** to your lender. That way, if your lender loses something like a W-2, you don't have to return to your accountant to ask for another copy. Or ask your human resources department for another copy -- or even worse, your wife.

You also want to check and double-check your application and HAMP Affidavit for errors. Why? Because your lender may tell you that you have made an error, but often won't tell you **exactly *where* you made your mistake**.

One day, a client brought me a letter that she had received from her lender.

The letter mentioned that she and her husband needed to send in a "properly-filled out" Home Affordable Hardship Affidavit, along with a list of other items. She couldn't believe it.

She didn't understand what was happening because she had sent recent W-2s, paystubs and bank statements.

The letter mentioned "a properly completed" Hardship Affidavit.

She claimed that everything was complete.

And at first glance, my client's Affidavit seemed complete.

However, please remember this simple strategy when dealing with bank and government employees. They require that **every line be filled out and legible**. Keeping this rule in mind, I looked back and noticed mistakes that seemed to jump out at me.

Mistake #1: Failure to write your name. Many homeowners make this mistake. They assume that since their bank generated the application and it has their loan number on it; they no longer have to write down their names. Not true. Fill out everything and you will avoid getting it rejected.

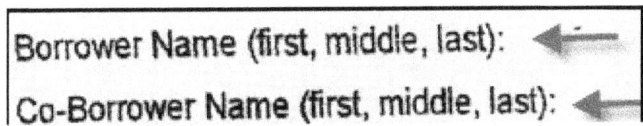

Mistake #2: Failure to write legibly. When I first looked at this Affidavit, it appeared that one borrower was born in 1940, however, that was just an assumption because a coffee stain blotted out the exact year. The person may have been born in 1940 or 1943 for all I know. Don't assume that people can read your mind!

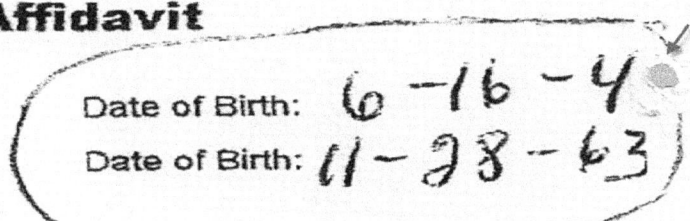

Mistake #3: Check all the boxes on each line that applies to you and/or the co borrower. Below, do you notice that one of the boxes for the co borrower should have been checked? The main borrower checked "Yes". But what about the co-borrower? A simple mistake like not checking a box can cause the affidavit to be rejected!

Yes ☒   No ☐   Yes ☐   No ☐   My cash reserves cover basic living

More Common Mistakes Probably the most persistent mistake I've seen involves gathering **Bank Statements**. Homeowners generally assume that the lender only wants the first two pages of the bank statement – after all, these are the pages with all the important numbers on them. Not true. The "Servicer" of your loan (your lender) wants all the pages of a bank statement -- even the ones that you don't think are important. So many times, this means that you will have to **copy both sides** of the bank statement and include pages that don't seem important. How to tell if you have all the pages? **Check the lower right hand corner** of the statement and make sure that it matches the number of pages you send.

Filling out IRS Form 4506T-EZ.

Most loan mod companies will require that you fill out IRS Form 4506T EZ. This form allows the bank to compare the income that you claim that you make with what you actually reported to the IRS. Fill out this form correctly the first time, and you won't have a problem. Here are three tips.

✓ **Tip #1. If you are married, and filed a joint return, both names should go on the same form. It's best that both signatures are on it but it's okay if only one person signs it.** Write your name and address in the boxes, and don't forget to include toinclude BOTH of your social security numbers.

✓ **Tip #2: If you are NOT married and have a co-borrower, than use separate forms**. Write your name and address in the boxes as well as your social security number. Need an additional form? Search for this federal tax form online or at http://www.irs.gov

✓ **Tip#3: Your lender's name, address and telephone number will go on Line 5 of the form – which you can find on your latest mortgage payment coupon or year-end statement.**

See the sample filled-in 4506T-EZ on the following page.

Note: Lenders rarely want more than one year. So on Line 6, you will just write the LAST year's tax return. If this is July 2011, you would enter "2010".

Question: What if I forgot to file or I showed very little on last year's taxes?

Answer: You may need to file or amend your Federal taxes! Remember, the bank will use the information that you provided to the IRS to verify your income. In some cases, it may be easier to amend your Federal tax return, and then apply for your loan modification.

If you don't have the forms needed to amend your taxes, visit www.irs.gov and download Form 1040X.

Strategy#4: Use a "KISS" Hardship Explanation

Ideally, you should be able to write a **brief** hardship explanation on your Making Home Affordable *Affidavit. **Example: "illness in the family."**

Keep it simple, sweetie!

(*The Affidavit is the paperwork that you will receive after you send in your Making Home Affordable Application.)

So you will first fill out the HAMP application and include financials. After a few weeks you will receive the HAMP **Affidavit**, and send in more recent financials. You will then be given a trial payment to make and then finally, you will receive your final Loan modification papers that you will have notarized.

Also, if your lender is NOT part of the Making Homes Affordable Program, you will still need to create a hardship letter. Remember, keep it simple.

✓ **Do NOT write "See Attached" on the form** and then include a 10 page letter with pictures of you and your wife with the kids and their pets. Why? Because Lenders lose stuff.

So you don't want to wait for three months to get an answer only to find out that they lost the hardship letter and now you'll have to start all over. This happens all too often. So just keep it simple and don't send them any attachments.

Here are some Kiss examples

- **Financial hardship**. My hours got cut in half because the local naval yard shut down. Nobody in town is able to find work.

- **Divorce/Separation**. My wife left me. I have put an ad in the newspaper for a boarder, but I have not been able to find one.

- **Increased family size.** My wife just had a baby and because we can't afford to pay a babysitter, my wife is staying at home to care for the baby.

- **Illness in family**. My elderly mother has dementia and no health insurance so my wife quit her job and we moved into mom's house to take care of her.

Strategy #5: Add Comparable Sales Data

A CMA and it stands for **"comparative market analysis"**.

It is used by real estate agents to tell owners what their property is worth.

Do NOT use it with the Making Home Affordable applications, **but DO use** it if your loan does NOT qualify for the Making Homes Affordable website. A CMA form often comes in handy when negotiating principal debt reductions with those lenders, too. Why? Because it offers *specific* details about the prices that three homes have sold for in the area. These prices are **specific details** that can be verified by the lender online. The point is... be specific.

Reason for hardship: Because the economy is bad, my hours have been cut and I can't find another job. Homes in my area are selling from **$216,000 to $227,000 (see the attached CMA form)** and I owe **$378,543**. If I can't get my principle debt reduced along with my payment, I will have to walk away. Then we'll both lose.

Question: What is the best way to find out how much homes are selling for in your area? Answer: **Buy your favorite realtor a cup of coffee from Starbucks**. You know what I mean. Schmooze her. Buy her a gift card at Starbucks and offer it as a form of appreciation for providing you these specifics that will help the rest of your hardship letter sound more believable.

Strategy#6: Help Explain "the Reason Why"

To be convinced of something, Harvard social psychologist Ellen Langer says that **most people like to have a reason "why"**.

Langer conducted an experiment where ten people were standing in line to use a library copy machine. An experimenter would rush in, and ask if she could cut in line to use the copier. Guess what? 60% of the people said, "Yes, cut in line."

But when the experimenter asked if she could jump in line "because I have to make some copies" she was allowed to proceed 93% of the time.

That's amazing, isn't it? **93% of the time**.

What makes this experiment significant is because of the high percentage of people standing in line who were also there to make copies. What was the percentage of people standing in line to make copies?

It was 100%, right? Everybody standing in line wanted to make copies!

Yet when repeating the experiment **without** using the word "because" Langer found that only **60%** of the people standing in line would comply.

Langer concluded **that people like to have a reason for what they do and that using the word, "because" is a powerful way to persuade someone!**

This is an important concept because it shows that you will be more effective when you use the word "because". (I couldn't resist doing that to you!) ;-)

Remember that lenders are skeptics who want to see proven facts, statistics and hard information to back up what you're saying. They'll want you to **provide matching details with the reason why**.

In other words, if you are trying to convince the lender that you have experienced a hardship "because" your girlfriend has left and took all your savings from your bank account, then document it by showing a bank statement with **less** money in your savings account – not MORE than the old amount!

Some people have done this. (And no, it wasn't me when I did my own loan modification!)

Or if you claim in a letter that you're broke "because" your employer has cut back your hours, then enclose a paycheck stub that shows **fewer hours** and a lower income– NOT more hours and a higher income. Sheesh.

This may sound like common sense, but as Voltaire once quipped, "Common sense is not so common." Offer concrete, matching details that give the reason why. Your mortgage modification will become stronger when it is accompanied by "because" accompanied with a few concrete details. (Example: the "competitive market analysis" showing what other homes are selling for?)

Now that we have mastered these six strategies, let's move on to review three terrific tips that just might help push you over into "Approval-Land".

Three Terrific Tips

Tip#1: Use a "Contributor" Instead of a "Co-Signer".

If the income on a Financial Statement is insufficient to qualify, most people will think about asking Mom or Dad to be a **co-signer**. After all, you know what the definition of a co-signer is, don't you?

Co-signer: A form of endearment, when foreclosure is imminent, directed towards a solvent relative.

The idea is good, to add additional income to the loan. The problem is that the added debt of the co-signer *can make matters even worse! Why?* **Because the debt of a co-signer MUST be included in the qualifying calculations!**

A **better way** is to have a person agree to be a "**contributor**". The lender won't use all of the income of the contributor, usually only 70% of it, **but the DEBTS of the contributor are NOT counted.**

How Using a Contributor Works

If you are acting as a contributor to a household, you will need to write a brief letter that explains the situation. In addition, proof of payment will need to accompany the letter. For example, if the Contributor writes a letter stating that he contributes $450 a month, the lender will want to see 3 cancelled checks as well as proof of current employment. The homeowner would then show three bank statements proving that the homeowner puts this money in the bank. In addition, the contributor should sign a letter stating that he willingly pays the contribution, and have the letter notarized.

Date:

To Whom It May Concern,

My name is Timothy Montana and I help out with Jim and Dorothy Merino's household. They own a ranch and I live with them and contribute $650 per month. I have told them that I am willing to stay with them until December 31, 2016. Attached please find my last three cancelled checks to them along with 2 of my normal paystubs. I am willing to do this because Dorothy is my niece. I hope this helps you.

Sincerely,

Timothy Montana   date
                    AND

To Whom It May Concern,

My name is Dorothy Merino and I receive a check for $650 each month from my uncle to contribute to our household. My uncle, Tim Montana lives with us and helps us by doing odd chores and babysitting. Attached please find my last three month's bank statements, showing that I regularly deposit his $650 assistance. Please let me know if you need anything else from me as I will gladly provide it.

Dorothy Merino   date

Tip#2: Use a Room Rental Form for Cash income, but deposit the Cash.

If you're in foreclosure and you're trying to save your home, you will do anything to make money. But how do you explain to a lender that you regularly earn cash money each week by cleaning houses while wearing a sexy French-maid outfit? (Especially if you're a man!) Or what if your income is generated by recycling, doing garage sales, selling baseball cards on Ebay – or all of the above? How can you convince the lender that the money coming into your bank account will occur repeatedly each month? Answer: a Room- rental agreement will often do the trick: **provided that the lender can verify that the money on the room rental agreement matches your bank statement.** So structure it like the contributor in Tip #1.

✓ **If you fail to deposit the money into the bank, and only give the lender the room rental agreement, this isn't going to work and the lender isn't going to accept it as verifiable income.** So use a Room Rental Agreement. Example, John makes $500 in cash by recycling. He gives the cash to his girlfriend Cindy who writes a check to John for $500. John deposits the money in his bank account. Cindy's **cancelled checks and John's bank statements** prove to the lender that John makes the $500 each month.

✓ **Note:** if you send Online bank statements, be sure that **your account number** shows up on your printout. Here is a sample room rental agreement.

ROOM RENTAL AGREEMENT

This Agreement is between_____ (Property Provider) and

_____ (Tenant)

For the rental of a room located at

_____.

The monthly rent is $_____, payable on the _____ day of every month.

A security deposit of $_____, including Last Month's Rent (Yes No), paid on

_____

(date), shall be refunded by Property Provider within 21 days following Tenant's move-out, less any appropriate and reasonable charges for cleaning and/or for damages caused by Tenant and/or Tenant's guests.

With 30 days written notice to Tenant, Property Provider may raise the rent, alter the terms of the agreement, or terminate the tenancy; 60 days written notice will be given to terminate the tenancy if Tenant has resided on the premises for at least one (1) year. Conversely, the Tenant MUST give Property Provider 30 days written notice of intent to quit the premises.

Property Provider agrees to provide the following:

 Electricity___ Gas ____ DSL/Internet Service___

 Trash Removal_____ Water _____ Other _____

 Cable TV____ Gardener_____ Other _____

Property Provider and Tenant agree to honor the following House Rules and any additional written Rules attached:

_____No smoking inside the premises.

_____No Pets.

Room Maintenance and Privacy: Tenant shall maintain room in a safe, clean and sanitary condition. Other than in emergency situations, Property Provider may enter room to initiate repairs only after giving Tenant 24-hour advance written notice.

In case of emergency, Tenant authorizes Property Provider to contact:

Name/Relationship:_____

Phone:_____ Email:_____

Name/Relationship:_____

Phone:_____ Email:_____

By initialing as provided, Tenant acknowledges the receipt of the following documents (copies of which are attached hereto,) and are incorporated herein by reference:

_____ House Rules _____ Megan's Law

_____ Inventory & Condition Report _____ Furniture Inventory & Condition Report

_____ Repair / Replacement Agreement _____ Lead Paint Disclosure

_____ Maintenance Request Form _____ Inventory of Personal Property

_____ Other: _____ _____ Other: _____

The undersigned have read the foregoing Lease prior to execution & acknowledge receipt of a copy.

Dated this _____ day of _____, of the year _____

Tenant(s) Signature(s):

_____

1st Tenant   Date

_____

2nd Tenant   Date

Property Provider's Signature:

_____

Full Name   Date

Tip#3: Amend Your Federal Tax Return!

If you are self-employed, possibly you were too aggressive on taking tax deductions last year, and now you're short of income and can't qualify. If so, consider amending your taxes by filling out Form 1040X. It may cost less to pay the additional taxes and will probably help improve your chances for a successful loan modification! Important: if possible, hand-carry the amended pages to the nearest IRS office and have the IRS stamp them. Then send a copy of the stamped pages to your lender.

Loan Modification **Consultants Beware**

Some loan modification specialists make big money by modifying loans, however, these specialists often need to have a real estate license to do so. In California, modifying loans **without** a real estate license is a crime punishable with a maximum fine of $5,000 or up to one-year imprisonment. A business entity may be fined $10,000. The State Real Estate Commissioner also has regulatory authority to impose administrative fines for unlicensed real estate activity.

✓ Also, in California, the law does NOT allow a loan mortgage consultant to take "advance" fees. What this means to you is that a consultant MUST be paid **AFTER** the fact. The reason for the **NO ADVANCE FEE** policy is because the state doesn't want a consultant to take the owner's money and disappear. Or take the money and not do anything - - which has sadly happened in the past.

✓ Some states allow unlicensed individuals to get paid referral fees from loan modification consultants. If your state allows you to do so, use a Finder's Fee form to protect yourself. There is a Finder's Fee form at www.short-sales1-2-3.com/loanmodforms.html – this form is structured so even if a homeowner decides to sell or rent a home, you may get paid a finder's fee too.

Is this legal? Well, some people make money offering **"secretarial services"**. After all, not everyone owns a fax machine or has access to one. Kinko's charges $2 per page for faxing a document, why can't you? Most accountants disappear after tax season so finding one to type up a simple Profit and Loss Statement isn't always easy. You could do it, as a "secretarial service" as long as you didn't offer any tax advice. The homeowner would give you the numbers, and you could type them in a Profit & Loss form. If you are PAYING somebody to do a loan modification for you, there should be three forms.

1.   **L.O.A – Letter of Authorization**. This form allows a third party to act on behalf of the borrower/owner. Some loan modification lenders now require this form to be notarized. Basically this form allows the consultant to talk to the bank about your loan situation. Note: in the state of California, this should NOT be a power of attorney form.

2.   **Consultant Fee Agreement**. This form sets out the terms and fees for the person who is doing a loan modification.

3. **The Financial Analysis Statement or Budget** This document is probably the most important part of the puzzle. It must be filled out completely, signed by the owner(s) and sent back to the lender. What if I am doing my own modification?

Great, it's time to talk about your budget and/or financial statement.

Completing the Budget or Financial Analysis Form

Probably the most important step of a successful loan modification is completing either a financial analysis form – or budget. The two words- budget and financial analysis form (often used interchangeably by lenders) will often strike fear in the hearts of most owners but you've got nothing to fear from these forms.

The **Financial Analysis Form** looks more like a loan application and is very detailed. It can be several pages long. It typically looks like a loan application.

A Budget is easier to do because **no account numbers** are required. This is what is found on the HAMP application! There is a list of common expenses that are paid each month by the owner. The items on the budget will look something like this:

Income
Mortgage Amts.
Homeowner Insurance
Automobile loan
Automobile Insurance
Gasoline
Credit cards
Utilities
Telephone
Medical
Groceries/Food
Entertainment/Vacations
Child care
Clothing
Misc

On the next page you will find a sample filled-in budget.

JIM PATTON'S FILLED-IN BUDGET	
Number of Dependents	3
Monthly Net Income: Owner	$4,410
Monthly Income Co-owner:	0
Mortgage#1: (includes taxes & insurance)	$1,867
Homeowner Dues	$30
Insurance (auto, health,life)	$98
Automobile loan	$175
Automobile expenses (gas, maintenance)	$300
Credit cards	$88
Utilities	
Gas	$35
Water	$45
Power	$85
Trash	$35
Cable TV:	$50
Telephone:	$50
Internet:	$20
Medical	0
Groceries/Food	$400
Entertainment/Vacations	0

✓ **I'm going to let you in on a little secret – the budget doesn't** *have to be letter-perfect.*

The lender isn't overly concerned about getting every single number done with 100% accuracy. It's okay to "guestimate". However, if you have 10 children and only put down that you have 3, the **lender is going to notice** that discrepancy via your Federal Tax Returns. Notice that the entries for medical, clothing and vacations on Jim Patton's budget are a big fat ZERO. Again, these items can be checked on his Federal return.

What the lender really wants to see is that you follow these **Seven Simple Rules**.

✓ Rule#1: *Expenses* Cannot Exceed *Income* Or Your Loan Modification *Will Always Be Declined.*

If you notice Jim Patton's budget it shows a TOTAL INCOME of $4,410.

with a TOTAL DEBT of $3,238

The difference between them is **$1,132** dollars – not a lot of money --yet the loan modification was approved. The first loan was recast at $1,434 which included his property taxes and insurance. Now what if Jim had a 2nd loan? Would he have to fill out the same modification paperwork for the 2nd loan? Yes. So make a copy of it.

Note that Jim's expenses **did NOT** exceed his income. Normally you don't want to shave the numbers too close or the lender may ask for additional income. This was not a HAMP loan and each lender is different, but it serves as a good example for what lenders aim to achieve with a loan modification.

If the expenses DO exceed the income, the owner is declined. He may be told to leave the property or do a short sale. For a loan modification to be successful, the homeowner should have a few extra dollars left over. How much? Most lenders won't tell you, but keep this in mind.

After the loan modification has been agreed upon, the lender will want to feel comfortable that you will be able to stay current with the new payment arrangement and won't be bothering him again. So don't shave the budget numbers too close! Make a payment arrangement that you will be able to keep.

Because lenders want homeowners to be able to stay current, most HAMP lenders will wish to see a 31 -38% debt to income ratio. So let's talk about **DEBT RATIO** for a minute. We'll use the Jim Patton example from page 47.

Whenever a lender talks about a **ratio,** think back to 6th grade math. That's where you learned to calculate a ratio. How do you calculate a ratio? You divide the **BIG number** into the **LITTLE number**.

The big number = is Jim Patton's big monthly income. $4,410

The little number= is his monthly payment -- $1,434

1,434 divided by 4,410 = **0.3251** or a **33% housing debt ratio**.

For a TOTAL debt ratio, we add Jim's revolving debt: his monthly homeowner fee of $30, auto loan and credit cards. The total is $293.

$293 + $1,434 = $1,727

So $1,727 divided by $4,410 = **0.3916 total debt ratio.**

Note: some lenders will approve as high as a 45% total debt ratio on a case-by-case basis. A nurse fresh out of nursing school, for example, might be approved on a higher total debt ratio because her earnings may move higher in the next few years.

Example 2:

Homeowner Maggie makes $3,750 per month.

Her total monthly housing payment is $1,000.

$3,750/ $1,000 = .26 Her housing debt ratio = 26%

Since .26 is less than .38, so far so good. Her modification might be approved.

However, **Total debt ratio** includes Maggie's credit cards and car payments.

Maggie has one car payment of $500 and two credit cards totally $136 so her total debt is $1,000 + $500 + $136= $1,636.

$3750/$1,636 = .4362. **The lender will round up and say her TOTAL debt ratio is .44%**

Since .44 is greater than .38, Maggie's modification **might** be **declined**. What is the maximum debt Maggie can go? Answer: call the lender to find out! Often it's 42%.

- Yearly Gross Income = $45,000 / Divided by 12 = $3,750 per month income.

  $3,750 Monthly Income x .38 = $1,425 maximum total debt.

So if Maggie isn't approved, what can she do? She either needs to lose her car payment or add additional income. Perhaps Maggie can turn in her car and buy a cheaper one? Or rent out a bedroom? **Or find a contributor to help out with the expenses**?

Let's suppose that Maggie's aunt is willing to be a contributor. Maggie's aunt makes $3,000 per month. As a contributor **the lender will only use 70%** of the aunt's income or $2,100. But that extra income will be enough for Maggie to qualify. Or, let's suppose that Maggie rented out one bedroom for $450 per month. Therefore her total monthly income= $3,750 + $450 = $4,200. And $4,200/$1,636 = 38% so her modification would be approved! Maggie just needs to show three months bank statements plus a room rental agreement to document the additional income.

✓ Rule #2: Lenders Calculate Using a Gross Monthly Income

Most paystubs will give two figures, a GROSS and a NET monthly income.

On a paycheck, the gross income might be **$1,495** per month.

Less Federal Withholding: 98.10

Less OASDI 92.69

Less Medicare 21.68

Less State Withholding: 10.52

Less State SDI 11.96

Total Deductions: 234.95

And a **Net Income** of **$1,260** per month

For a loan modification, the HAMP program uses the GROSS figure of $1,495; or 31% of the gross. But some lenders (such as Credit Unions) will sometimes use net income when doing loan modifications.

If in doubt, be sure to let them know when you fill out the budget or financial statement. Write: This is my NET income in the side margin. Also, it doesn't hurt to call your lender and ask!

GETTING PAID WEEKLY

Question: What if the owner gets paid $1,260 weekly?

Answer: When using a weekly income, multiply the amount $1,260 x 52

(as there are 52 weeks in a year.) Do not multiply $1,260 x 4 and then by 12.

Question: Why not multiply the $1,260 by 4 (as there are 4 weeks in a month) and then by 12? (there are 12 months in a year.)

Answer: Because the income will be substantially lower when you do it this way. Watch what happens.

$1,260 x 52 weeks = $65,520

$1,260 x 4 weeks = $5,040 x 12 months = $60,480

So I am going to get a higher monthly income by using the first approach. $65,520 divided by 12 = $5,460 per month.

Now if the homeowner has 2 weeks of vacation, I'll multiply by 50.

$1,260 x 50 weeks = $63,000/ 12 = $5,250 per month.

Remember: MOST lenders are like Don Corleone. They want to see all your money that's coming in.

Question: What if the owner doesn't have pay stubs? He gets paid in cash or is self-employed?

Answer: If the owner gets paid in cash or is self-employed, he will usually need to show 6 months bank statements, plus provide his last year's taxes and a current year-to-date Profit and Loss statement.

Sample Profit & Loss Statement

Below is an example of what a profit and loss statement looks like.

Profit and Loss Statement			
December 2009 – February 2010			
Andy's Household Furniture			
1234 Main Street			
Santa Clarita, CA. 91321			
	December	**January**	**February**
Income	$1,548.00	$1,643.00	$1,520.00
Other			
Total	$1,548.00	$1,643.00	$1,520.00
Expenses			
Gasoline	47	61	36
Cell Phones	30	30	30
Space Rent	200	200	200
Small tools		35	
Total	277	326	266
Net Income	$1,271.00	$1,317.00	$1,254.00
Total Average Three Month Net Profit: $3,842.00/3 = $1,280.67			

This information is true and correct to the best of my knowledge.

Joe Schmoe   date

✓ **Be sure to sign and date the profit and loss statement.** Note: a Profit and Loss Statement doesn't have to be made by an accountant or be on a professional letterhead, but it must be signed. It should also have a statement above the signature that states that the information is true and correct. Don't forget that statement!

Rule #3: Sort out Expenses. This rule applies to **non-HAMP** loan modifications. Many homeowners will lump $4,385 a month in bills all together. This makes it difficult to comprehend their true financial situation. So try to sort things out for the lender by clarifying *the installment debt* from the rest of the household expenses.

Question: What is installment debt?

> **Answer:** Installment debt means any type of payment made on installment – so home and auto loan payments, credit card payments, student loan payments, child support and alimony payments (as well as legal judgments) all fit into this debt category.

In fact, some lenders may have you further separate the monthly mortgage payments from all other monthly installment debt.

Two monthly mortgage pmts	**$2,250 + $500 = $2,750**
Other monthly installment debt	**Car pmt and Credit cards: $635**
Other monthly living expenses:	**$1,000**
Total Monthly Expenses:	**$4,385**

What about auto insurance? Insurance is NOT considered installment debt. It's considered a normal household expense. .

Tip: Convince the lender that after the payment has been modified you will be able to safely afford the NEW payment for a *long* time in the future.

Rule #4: Whenever Possible, Write the Loan Number on Everything You Send – Using A LARGER Than Normal Sized Font.

Lenders receive lots of documents, and small font-sizes tend to get squished by fax machines. So if possible, **make your loan number larger** by using a size 20 font or larger. Do NOT use a size 12 or 10 size font.

1234567 not 1234567

Rule#5: Unless Advised Differently, Fax or Upload All Completed Information *At The Same Time* To The Lender.

Gather copies of all the documentation required on the Mortgage Modification checklist.

The Federal tax information, bank statements and last month's paystubs, etc.

You will fax or upload them to the Lender along with the signed Financial Statement and hardship letter.

In other words, you'll want to fax or upload EVERYTHING AT ONE TIME and remember to make a fax cover sheet with the loan number in larger than normal font type. If the lender has a special cover sheet – be sure to use it!

If you are ONLY waiting for a more recent paystub, fax or upload everything immediately without waiting.

Rule#6: Save Your Money.

In order to approve the loan modification, the lender often will require that the owner continue to make their payments and may even require a **"down payment"** or **"Contribution."**

This can be as little as $500 **or as great as 3 months payments**. So it's important to save, save, save!

Rule#7: In Real Estate *Everything* is Negotiable!

I have said earlier that lenders have rules about what is acceptable and what is not. They will usually make things difficult for owners and some lenders may not even do a loan modification for a homeowner who is too far behind - - however, don't bank on that. (Pun intended) **Lenders can and do break their own rules!**

One homeowner did a loan modification two years ago, and wanted to apply for a second modification. He was told by his bank that he couldn't. I suggested that he apply again under the HAMP program. Guess what happened? He got approved under Hamp.

 A homeowner with a rental house was told by the lender that they would only do modifications on primary residences. Guess what? He got a second home approved on a loan modification that wasn't a HAMP.

You name it, and rules have probably been broken. So even if you have been told "No" by somebody, don't be afraid to give it a try.

you on how we may be able to help you overcome the mortgage pay
Although <u>we've determined that you are not eligible</u> for the *Home
Program*, we're pleased to let you know about a different program
you.

iilable to you
ligible for a different program that can help relieve your mortgage
s alternate program is designed for homeowners like you who did 1
ements under the *Home Affordable Modification Program.* Throu
our mortgage payments and modification terms will be similar to 1
Modification Program.

Remember: in real estate, ***everything is negotiable***.

A Word about Bank Accounts

Please be aware that lenders can (and do) check all bank accounts that are registered via the **primary** social security number registered on the account.

Therefore, if Julie Simmons is listed as a co-signor to her mother's account, she doesn't need to include that account on her application. As long as mom's name and social is the primary account holder, it's not really Julie's money to spend.

After all, maybe Julie can't access that money without her mom's consent and/or until mom has passed away. So only list the bank accounts where the owner is registered as the **primary** account holder.

Communicate with Your Lender

Okay, let's get back to business. After I have faxed or uploaded all of my financial information to the lender along with the HAMP Application or HAMP Affidavit, what happens next? **Answer: you'll want to frequently call or fax your lender**.

1. Call the lender to make certain that they've received the complete package. This is an important phone call to make. There have been instances where people mistakenly believed that action was taking place on a file only to find out later that the package they sent was misplaced or the fax was never received by the lender in the first place!

- TIP: whenever you communicate with your lender be as friendly and helpful as possible. Listen closely and give the lender the information that they request. Nothing more.

- A loan modification is a business deal and it should be treated with that kind of regard. Stick to the facts and do not embellish, bellyache or exaggerate.

2. Maintain a **Positive Attitude**. People who work for the bank are often speaking with lots of angry and frustrated homeowners. I might be remembered better if I crack a corny joke, so I'll usually do that, or just ask how the weather is, or ask which NBA basketball team they like, NFL football or baseball.

The key is to call frequently but be patient and friendly – even if this is the fourth time you have faxed the entire package to them!

People have asked: "How did you get your file moved to the front of the line?" and I usually can't point my finger at any one thing that I've done. But maybe it's because I call and fax often and the lender knows that when I call I'm not going to yell at them.

Why send a fax? Because it has to be filed. So if somebody is lazy and they know that I am going to be faxing them something, they'll keep my file on top of the stack!

- In any case, be nice to people. You catch more flies with honey than vinegar, right?

Crack jokes about the weather, the basketball game or movie you saw. Try to personalize your discussions and you may discover that you get better results.

Third: With **non-HAMP loans**, I'll often send out a **"Thank You"** note. Yep, I will send one to the woman I spoke to on the phone that will read something like this.

Dear Cindy,

Just a note to say that it was a pleasure chatting with you on the phone. You seemed like a very pleasant person. Please let me know if there is anything else you need. I'll be happy to provide you whatever paperwork you need to get this file approved. My clients really want to stay in their home!

Warmest regards,

Bob Boog

Three Reasons Why I Send Thank You Notes.

Reason#1: To kiss up to my lender contact. There, I said it.

Reason #2: Because people who work at banks doing loan modifications are over-worked and under appreciated, I want the bank person to remember me, return my calls and approve the loan modifications that I send. Would you remember me if I was the only one who sent you a little personalized thank you card? (Say "yes").

Reason#3: I have also found that sending out <u>my personalized, trademarked "We Like You" cards</u> is great for creating Good Karma and gaining future business too. Why? Because it is estimated that 25% of homeowners who get their loans modified fail to keep their payments current. So if my clients need help in the future to sell their home, who might they call? Hopefully me.

How to Torpedo a Loan Modification

I just mentioned that a good percentage of homeowners who modify their loans successfully will fail to keep their agreements, but what about the people who start doing a loan modification but never complete it? Approximately 25% fail. Some fall short because they do not properly document their income. Others do not make the grade because they don't make their trial payments on time. And others do not succeed because **somebody convinces them to do a short sale**. That's right. Some smart real estate person may try to switch you in mid-stream. Don't fall for this. Because if you change from a loan modification to a short sale, your **lender will think that you are just stalling for time and they will immediately foreclose!** In addition, you will lose out on the $3,000 HAFA relocation money! So wait to get denied. Then do a short sale.

Principal Debt Reduction

According to the Los Angeles Times (August 21, 2010) nearly half of all people who will attempt to modify their loan(47%) will drop out. Why? Some fail to fill out the forms correctly or don't qualify – that's how this guide came about. For many people, though reduced financial circumstances have kept many folks over their heads in debt. What can be done about it? Most experts will tell owners to save money, make extra cash by renting a room, or selling items on eBay. Yada, yada, yada.

The only sure-fire solution for getting rid of debt is **filing for bankruptcy**. You may not want to hear that, but it's true. Chapter 7 bankruptcy is the best way to reduce debt.

So the idea would be to modify your first loan, then file for a Chapter 7 bankruptcy. Check with an attorney. Who knows? You may be able to include your equity-line-of-credit that people have been harassing you morning, noon and night with those annoying automated phone calls from some telephone call center in Pakistan! Hmm. What if I want to avoid the stigma of bankruptcy and the 7-10 years of bad credit. Isn't there another solution? Yes.

I have helped some homeowners reduce their principal debt on loans without filing for bankruptcy, but I've had mixed results, so it's not guaranteed. Sometimes it works, and sometimes it doesn't. Please note: I have only gotten results with this method in **non-Hamp** modifications. It's called a Short Loan Modification. Again, feel free to Google it and see if other people are more successful.

When you do a short loan modification, you are asking the lender to break their contract and reduce the principal balance. Many banks have a problem with this because they are afraid if word gets out, everyone will want the same thing! So you have to keep this tip under your hat! When the same bank holds both loans – the bank may modify both loans by consolidating the second loan into the first. Example: Bill and Mary have a first loan of $280,000 with BofA and a second loan of $40,000 with BofA . So they owe $320,000 on a house that's worth $208,000. They send BofA a letter along with their loan modification, requesting that both loans be modified because houses in their area are currently selling for $208,000. To their surprise, when their loan modification documents arrive, both loans have been consolidated into one. Their principal balance is now $224,000. Note: if your second loan is with a DIFFERENT company than your first loan, the second lender MUST give you a loan modification if your first loan is approved by the Hamp program.

- ✓ Important: when you do a short loan modification, expect the lender to reduce the principal balance by about 10%- 20%. Why? That is the loss amount that is generally acceptable with doing a short sale.
- ✓ You will want to write a brief letter to explain why. I'm not going to tell you how to word the letter exactly, **but you will want to use the word "bankruptcy" in that letter.** It's not exactly a threat, but most banks don't want to go through the time and hassle of a bankruptcy court. So if you say something to the effect, "As you can see from the comparable sales on the attached form, houses in our area have dropped in value significantly. And if we can't get some kind of debt reduction, we will be forced to file for bankruptcy—and/or walk away."
- ✓ You will want to include a CMA form –(comparable market analysis). It shows the lender what the prices of homes are selling for in the area.

Constant Communication Continued

If more than a week has passed and you have not received a fax, phone call, email or other communication from the lender, call the lender to find out the status OR send them a fax. Why a fax? A fax has to be handled and filed. If you send a fax everyday, the person will either want to get rid of your file because they have to keep putting stuff in it, or keep it on top to make it handy to reach for filing purposes.

I also use a little red-inked stamp that I had made at Staples. It works great, too. It just says **URGENT.** I stamp my cover sheet a few times with it, and write down what I am trying to accomplish. Example: Please send me a status report on loan# 1234567. Jones. **URGENT** So when calling or faxing the lender always reference the **LOAN NUMBER**.

Ask Specific Questions:

"Hi, my name is Bob Boog and I'm calling on Loan Number 66729. I was wondering if the Jenkins loan modification paperwork will be sent out on **Monday**, **September 15th**?" Usually with that specific question, I will get a "No, that one's not going to be ready until the September 21st." Or "No, we're still missing a paystub."

- Either way, by asking for a **specific** date, I'll find out exactly **what** is lacking or **when** the paperwork will be sent! Try it!

- **IMPORTANT: Most negotiators will not give out their email addresses, but if and when you are** communicating via *email*, **always remember to include the Loan Number and address in the subject line.**

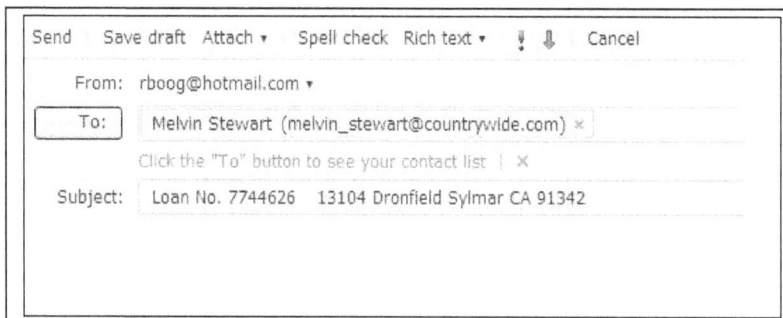

-
Send Save draft Attach ▾ Spell check Rich text ▾ ⬆ ⬇ Cancel	
From:	rboog@hotmail.com ▾
To:	Melvin Stewart (melvin_stewart@countrywide.com) ✕
	Click the "To" button to see your contact list ✕
Subject:	Loan No. 7744626 13104 Dronfield Sylmar CA 91342

Figure 1 Enter the loan number and address in the subject line of an email

Smart things to Say to the Lender

"My clients really want to stay in this home -- if they can."

"They are really trying to avoid filing for bankruptcy, if they can."

If the lender has come up with a payment, no matter what it is, I'll say:

"Hmm, is this the best you can do?"

"Is there a way that you could waive some of these late fees?"

"What if we made this a 40 year loan, would that change anything?"

"Can we try this at a 2% interest rate that is fixed for ten years?"

"What if we added another Contributor, would that help?"

"What if he/she sells her car?"

"Can I please get your employee identification number?"

Always Be Prepared

No one wants to lose their home to foreclosure and with information being exchanged, it is easy to forget things or miss the details. So write down things. Just my .02 worth.

Don't rely on your memory, it can fail you. Make sure you have **everything written out** in front of you. Never make a call without first reviewing your notes, and having a strategy already in place.

Question: Why do some loan modifications take so long?

Answer: Lenders are often overwhelmed with owners in the same situation. They are processing thousands of files each day. That's why it's important to stay upbeat and be persistent. It can sometimes take days just to get a return phone call from some loss mitigation units. But don't give up.

Remember to Make Timely Payments When You Are On the Trial Period. I can't stress this enough. If you are accepted on the Making Homes Affordable program and are issued trial payments, if you miss ONE payment, or make the payment on the 16th day of the month and not the 15th, the bank may reject your application. Or if they don't reject it, the payments may get recalculated **and then you might not qualify.** So please, seriously, you will make your life much easier if you make your payments on time. **Wire the payment -- or just call.** Most lenders are happy to take your payment over the telephone. So have your checkbook handy and be ready to read off the routing and account numbers.

What if I am in foreclosure and am tired of getting harassing phone calls?

Answer: You can register with the <u>"do not call" database</u> or you can write a letter like this one:

13 March 2009

Dear Sir or Madam:

Re: Account No: 123456   1353 Delaney Road, Newhall, Ca. 91321

I request that you **CEASE and DESIST** in your efforts to collect on the above referenced account. The owner, Gerald Van Camp is in the process of modifying his two mortgages. The value of this property is worth only a fraction of what he paid for it, and he is doing his best under trying circumstances.

You are hereby instructed **to cease collection efforts immediately** or face legal sanctions under applicable Federal and State law. Please have your loss mitigation department direct any and all calls to our office so that everyone can move ahead on this file.

PLEASE GIVE THIS LETTER THE PROMPT ATTENTION IT DESERVES.

Yours truly,

[Your name]

Please note, I can't promise that this letter will stop every phone call, but what is the intent of this book? To **increase your odds**, remember?

The FINAL Modification Agreement

- The final loan modification agreement will be sent to your house directly usually via UPS or Express Mail and the documents will need to be **notarized**. (Sometimes not.) But if so, be sure to **bring your driver's license** to the notary when you go to sign them. Ideally, go to the bank that made the loan or call them and they will often notarize the documents for free!

Pay close attention to the terms in the written modification agreement.   Is the address correct? (You might be surprised how often a wrong address shows up!)

✓ Are the interest rate and payment calculation correct?

✓ What are the provisions for the mortgage holder's recovery of delinquent interest and accrued fees? [Review both the method of recovery/repayment and the calculation of the total amount to be recovered.]

✓ What penalties take effect if the loan is not kept current? In some cases the lender will attempt to keep the foreclosure door open, thereby allowing for an accelerated foreclosure if the loan becomes delinquent again.

✓ If you find a discrepancy kindly bring it up to your lender, as most omissions or mistakes are simply that, and nothing more and can very easily be corrected.

✓ Most modification agreements have separate addendums that allow you to have the documents reviewed by an attorney. So it's a good idea to do so, or have an attorney's phone number on hand if wish to call with a question.

✓ Many addendums include a standard "No verbal agreement" addendum and an "Errors and Omissions" addendum. No biggie.

✓ Finally, after signing everything in front of a notary, the owner should send the completed written loan modification agreement to the lender. BE SURE TO KEEP A COPY OF IT!

BAC Home Loans Servicing, LP
Attn: Home Retention Division
4500 Amon Carter Blvd
Fort Worth, TX 76155

Bank of America 🇺🇸 Home Loans

Property Address:
Joe Homeowner
1234 Main Street
Newhall, Ca. 91321

Notice Date: 5/5/2010
Loan No.: 98776559
Please Return the Enclosed Documents By: 5/15/2010

Loan Modification
CLARITY COMMITMENT ™

Thank you for working with BAC Home Loans Servicing, LP, a subsidiary of Bank of America, N.A., on your current mortgage needs and for making your trial period mortgage payments. This summary is intended to be a clear and simple description of the final loan modification that we are pleased to offer you. Once you sign and return the enclosed Home Affordable Modification Agreement, you will have agreed to the new permanent loan modification. Please thoroughly review all the materials in the enclosed package to ensure you understand the details of this new agreement.

Summary of Your Modified Loan

Your new loan balance is $345,300.92. Past due interest, servicing expenses paid to third parties and escrow advances of $19,608.55 have been added to your principal balance to calculate this new loan balance. Unpaid late fees are not included in this amount and will be waived when your loan modification is finalized.

Your new interest rate that will be in effect for the first 5 years of your modified loan is 2.000%. This rate will annually increase by one percent a year thereafter until it reaches 5.000%. To further lower your monthly payment we have extended the length of your loan to 40 years and we have also deferred the repayment of $131,659.37 in principal to the end of the loan term. This deferred principal amount will be noninterest bearing and will also be due when you pay off the modified loan. Your new final payment date and maturity date is 5/01/2050.

Each month you make on-time payments, you may be eligible for incentive payments under the Home Affordable Modification Program to be applied to your principal balance on the 1st-5th anniversaries of the Trial Period Plan Effective Date, provided your loan does not become 90 days delinquent at any time.

Your New Mortgage Payments

Your new total modified monthly mortgage payments of $1,170.54 are made up of principal and interest of $646.96, and an initial escrow amount of $523.58. Escrow payments are collected for payment of items such as property taxes and insurance and may change. We will notify you of any adjustments to the total monthly payment.
Your total monthly payments will be due on the 1st of the month starting June 1, 2010.

Your interest rate will adjust to slowly bring your rate to 5% and your total monthly payments to $1,501.06, as shown in the schedule below. The amount of these payments will change if your escrow payment amount changes.

- Years 1-5, beginning 6/01/2010 the interest rate will be 2.000% with a total monthly payment of $1,170.54
- Years 6, beginning 6/01/2015, the interest rate will be 3.000% with a total monthly payment of $1,275.20
- Years 7, beginning 6/01/2016, the interest rate will be 4.000% with a total monthly payment of $1,385.67
- Years 8-40, beginning 6/01/2017, the interest rate will be 5.000% with a total monthly payment of $1,501.06

If you have questions regarding the Modification Agreement or the steps you must take to complete this process, please contact us at 1.877.422.1761 to speak with one of our home retention associates.

CMO 275

✓ You now have to make sure that **the Lender signs and records** it.

Remember: if your property is in foreclosure, the foreclosure will continue until the modification has **been recorded**, *and it will be* **YOUR** *responsibility to stay on top of the lender and trustee to see that this is done.* So don't fall asleep at the wheel. In other words, you may need to notify the **Trustee or attorney** handling the foreclosure proceedings directly as sometimes the Lender's left hand does not know what the right hand is doing. **The sheriff's sale will not be postponed until the lawyer/trustee receives word from the lender!**

✓ Have there been instances where the Lender failed to sign the written loan modification agreement and the property was sold at a foreclosure auction? **YES!** So it's very important to make sure that the lender has received the package back from you.

✓ **New Payment**. The owner will NOT receive a payment statement or coupon book immediately, and if he waits to get one, the new payment may be late. Or the new payment may be handled by a different billing department. So be proactive and **contact the bank about where to send the new payment.** Expect to send a WIRE or use your TELEPHONE to make the first payment and WRITE DOWN THE TRACKING NUMBER. Too many people start off on the wrong foot by waiting for the bank to send them a payment coupon. Don't be one of them!

Finally, if the loan modification through HAMP is declined you should contact a competent real estate attorney **as some lenders will look to foreclose faster than a microwave can heat up your leftovers.**

Should you hire an attorney to review the final loan modification agreement? It's up to you. If the terms seem different than what you had agreed upon, it may be money well spent. In other words, it may cost $300-$600 for an attorney to review the final documents. Still, it's a far cry from the attorney's normal fee of $2,500 -$4,500 for typical attorney loan modification services. So if it will bring you peace of mind, then BY ALL MEANS, DO IT!

Most banks don't want to fight a lawsuit and therefore, if you feel that your loan modification has been unfairly declined, do contact a lawyer. There may be violations of the Truth in Lending laws or other infractions that may be applicable in your case. It's up to you to fight for your family, so chose a lawyer with real estate experience and not just anybody from the phone book or Internet.

The End of the Road

This concludes this book. Thanks for reading it. I tried to make it brief and relevant. I hope you have found it useful. I'd like to publicly thank my wife Roxana for putting up with me staying in the office after hours to write it.

Because most people do not use ONE source for information on golf, growing roses or diet tips, why should loan modifications be any different? So please feel free to check around and see what other advice is available – especially at the <u>Making Homes Affordable website</u>. After all, stuff happens. Guidelines can change and what was once acceptable --might not be two months from now. Many authors have written, "If this book helps one person, then it has been worth it." I sincerely hope that it will be of assistance to you! Who knows? This knowledge may assist you to help someone else save their home too. You may become a "Rock Star" for another family! Because you were the one who saved the family's home from foreclosure and/or you helped to lower their payment! Sounds like a good Simpson's episode if nothing else!

It is said that in the Chinese written language, the symbol for **crisis** is the same symbol used for **opportunity**. Likewise, during this time of economic crisis, this little book may represent a real opportunity for you. But like a gift unopened, it will do nothing if you just let it sit unopened and do nothing.

After all, what use is a gift sitting unopened in a closet? The ball is in your court now. The Federal government stands ready, willing and able to help but you have to act before December 31, 2012. Are you ready to rock and roll, rock star?

Bob Boog

Valencia, California

Common Real Estate Things That Are Good To Know

Another way to figure DTI (Debt-to-income ratio): **A debt-to-income ratio (often abbreviated DTI) is the percentage of a consumer's monthly gross income that goes toward paying debts.**

The two main kinds of DTI are expressed as a pair using the notation x/y (for example, 28/36).

1. The first DTI, known as the **front ratio**, indicates the percentage of income that goes toward **housing costs**.

2. The second DTI, known as the **back end ratio**, indicates the percentage of income that goes toward **paying all recurring debt payments.**

Example: In order to qualify for a mortgage for which the lender requires a debt-to-income ratio of 28/36:

- Yearly Gross Income = $45,000 / Divided by 12 = $3,750 per month income.
  - **$3,750 Monthly Income x .28 = $1,050** allowed for housing expense.
  - **$3,750 Monthly Income x .36 = $1,350** allowed for housing expense plus recurring debt.

Deed in Lieu of Foreclosure:

The word "in Lieu" means "instead of". Therefore a "deed in lieu of Foreclosure" means the homeowner offers to give the lender a deed to his property in exchange for cancellation of the debt. It's like bringing the keys back to a car dealer to be released from the lien. The only problem is that most lenders still report a deed in lieu as a foreclosure on a credit report which defeats the purpose of doing this.

Short Sale: Where the lender allows a homeowner to sell the property at fair market value – usually for much less than what the homeowner paid for the property. The lender reduces the amount of the unpaid principal balance in order to do so. A short sale is beneficial because the lender has to "agree" to it and so it shows up on a credit report as "paid as agreed." The book, **Short Sales 1-2-3** discusses short sales in detail and if you wish to purchase a copy of it, you can find it at my website. [www.short-sales1-2-3.com/]

Forbearance Plan:

A forbearance plan is an option where the lender arranges a revised repayment plan. This could include a temporary reduction or suspension of monthly loan payments. They are often used in times of a natural disaster such as after Hurricane Katrina. Forbearance plans are usually just temporary – for a few months.

Repayment Plan:

Where a homeowner makes an agreement with the lender to make up the unpaid loan payments. Some lenders may require that up to 50% of the past due balance is to be paid. While this sounds great, in many cases this is just not possible. After all, if the owner had 50% of the past due balance, he probably would not be that far behind. Part of doing a loan modification is negotiating with a lender to work out a reasonable amount of money from the owner to bring the loan current.

Restructuring:

This is where a lender rolls any past-due amounts, including interest and escrow, into the unpaid principal balance Anything is negotiable. If the variable interest rate was adjusted, you may be able to have the rate adjusted back to the lower rate. This will not only help you get a lower monthly payment, but will also help pay off the home sooner than before. Remember, Federal legislation allows homeowners who negotiate loan modifications with lenders to escape income-tax liability for the amount forgiven.

Reinstatement:

Reinstatement is the total amount that is past due including late fees and attorney costs. Paying the past due balances will get your mortgage caught up immediately. There might be a huge amount of past-due fees which could include back payments, late fees and legal expenses. Reinstatement might be accomplished if you can promise a lump-sum to bring your payments to a current status by a specific date.

About the Author

Bob Boog is the owner/broker of Bob Boog Realty located in Newhall, Ca. A graduate of UCLA, he has been involved in real estate sales since 1978.

If you found this book especially useful or feel motivated to say thanks, you can do that by recommending it to a friend or neighbor.

Good luck, see you around the bend and remember:

"The purpose of fun is to have it."

Print Form

Making Home Affordable Program
Request For Modification and Affidavit (RMA)

MAKING HOME AFFORDABLE.gov

REQUEST FOR MODIFICATION AND AFFIDAVIT (RMA) page 1	COMPLETE ALL THREE PAGES OF THIS FORM

▶ Loan I.D. Number_____   ▶ Servicer _____

BORROWER	CO-BORROWER
Borrower's name	Co-borrower's name
Social Security number Date of birth	Social Security number Date of birth
Home phone number with area code	Home phone number with area code
Cell or work number with area code	Cell or work number with area code

I want to:	☐ Keep the Property	☐ Sell the Property	
The property is my:	☐ Primary Residence	☐ Second Home	☐ Investment
The property is:	☐ Owner Occupied	☐ Renter Occupied	☐ Vacant

Mailing address

Property address (if same as mailing address, just write same)   E-mail address

Is the property listed for sale? ☐ Yes ☐ No Have you received an offer on the property? ☐ Yes ☐ No Date of offer _____ Amount of offer $_____ Agent's Name: _____ Agent's Phone Number: _____ For Sale by Owner? ☐ Yes ☐ No	Have you contacted a credit-counseling agency for help ☐ Yes ☐ No If yes, please complete the following: Counselor's Name: _____ Agency Name: _____ Counselor's Phone Number: _____ Counselor's E-mail: _____
Who pays the real estate tax bill on your property? ☐ I do ☐ Lender does ☐ Paid by condo or HOA Are the taxes current? ☐ Yes ☐ No Condominium or HOA Fees ☐ Yes ☐ No $_____ Paid to: _____	Who pays the hazard insurance premium for your property? ☐ I do ☐ Lender does ☐ Paid by Condo or HOA Is the policy current? ☐ Yes ☐ No Name of Insurance Co.: _____ Insurance Co. Tel #: _____

Have you filed for bankruptcy? ☐ Yes ☐ No   If yes: ☐ Chapter 7 ☐ Chapter 13   Filing Date:_____
Has your bankruptcy been discharged? ☐ Yes ☐ No   Bankruptcy case number _____

Additional Liens/Mortgages or Judgments on this property:

Lien Holder's Name/Servicer	Balance	Contact Number	Loan Number

HARDSHIP AFFIDAVIT

I (We) am/are requesting review under the Making Home Affordable program.
I am having difficulty making my monthly payment because of financial difficulties created by (check all that apply):

☐ My household income has been reduced. For example: unemployment, underemployment, reduced pay or hours, decline in business earnings, death, disability or divorce of a borrower or co-borrower.	☐ My monthly debt payments are excessive and I am overextended with my creditors. Debt includes credit cards, home equity or other debt.
☐ My expenses have increased. For example: monthly mortgage payment reset, high medical or health care costs, uninsured losses, increased utilities or property taxes.	☐ My cash reserves, including all liquid assets, are insufficient to maintain my current mortgage payment and cover basic living expenses at the same time.

☐ Other:

Explanation (continue on back of page 3 if necessary): _____
_____

REQUEST FOR MODIFICATION AND AFFIDAVIT (RMA) page 2　　**COMPLETE ALL THREE PAGES OF THIS FORM**

INCOME/EXPENSES FOR HOUSEHOLD¹　　　　　Number of People in Household:

Monthly Household Income		Monthly Household Expenses/Debt		Household Assets	
Monthly Gross Wages	$	First Mortgage Payment	$	Checking Account(s)	$
Overtime	$	Second Mortgage Payment	$	Checking Account(s)	$
Child Support / Alimony / Separation²	$	Insurance	$	Savings/ Money Market	$
Social Security/SSDI	$	Property Taxes	$	CDs	$
Other monthly income from pensions, annuities or retirement plans	$	Credit Cards / Installment Loan(s) (total minimum payment per month)	$	Stocks / Bonds	$
Tips, commissions, bonus and self-employed income	$	Alimony, child support payments	$	Other Cash on Hand	$
Rents Received	$	Net Rental Expenses	$	Other Real Estate (estimated value)	$
Unemployment Income	$	HOA/Condo Fees/Property Maintenance	$	Other _____	$
Food Stamps/Welfare	$	Car Payments	$	Other _____	$
Other (investment income, royalties, interest, dividends etc.)	$	Other _____ _____	$	Do not include the value of life insurance or retirement plans when calculating assets (401k, pension funds, annuities, IRAs, Keogh plans, etc.)	
Total (Gross Income)	$	Total Debt /Expenses	$	Total Assets	$

INCOME MUST BE DOCUMENTED

¹Include combined income and expenses from the borrower and co-borrower (if any). If you include income and expenses from a household member who is not a borrower, please specify using the back of this form if necessary.
²You are not required to disclose Child Support, Alimony or Separation Maintenance Income, unless you choose to have it considered by your servicer.

INFORMATION FOR GOVERNMENT MONITORING PURPOSES

The following information is requested by the federal government in order to monitor compliance with federal statutes that prohibit discrimination in housing. You are not required to furnish this information, but are encouraged to do so. The law provides that a lender or servicer may not discriminate either on the basis of this information, or on whether you choose to furnish it. If you furnish the information, please provide both ethnicity and race. For race, you may check more than one designation. If you do not furnish ethnicity, race, or sex, the lender or servicer is required to note the information on the basis of visual observation or surname if you have made this request for a loan modification in person. If you do not wish to furnish the information, please check the box below.

BORROWER	☐ I do not wish to furnish this information	CO-BORROWER	☐ I do not wish to furnish this information
Ethnicity:	☐ Hispanic or Latino ☐ Not Hispanic or Latino	Ethnicity:	☐ Hispanic or Latino ☐ Not Hispanic or Latino
Race:	☐ American Indian or Alaska Native ☐ Asian ☐ Black or African American ☐ Native Hawaiian or Other Pacific Islander ☐ White	Race:	☐ American Indian or Alaska Native ☐ Asian ☐ Black or African American ☐ Native Hawaiian or Other Pacific Islander ☐ White
Sex:	☐ Female ☐ Male	Sex:	☐ Female ☐ Male

To be completed by Interviewer		Name/Address of Interviewer's Employer
This request was taken by:	Interviewer's Name (print or type) & ID Number	
☐ Face-to-face Interview ☐ Mail	Interviewer's Signature　　Date	
☐ Telephone ☐ Internet	Interviewer's Phone Number (include area code)	

REQUEST FOR MODIFICATION AND AFFIDAVIT (RMA) page 3   COMPLETE ALL THREE PAGES OF THIS FORM

ACKNOWLEDGEMENT AND AGREEMENT

In making this request for consideration under the Making Home Affordable Program, I certify under penalty of perjury:

1. That all of the information in this document is truthful and the event(s) identified on page 1 is/are the reason that I need to request a modification of the terms of my mortgage loan, short sale or deed-in-lieu of foreclosure.

2. I understand that the Servicer, the U.S. Department of the Treasury, or their agents may investigate the accuracy of my statements and may require me to provide supporting documentation. I also understand that knowingly submitting false information may violate Federal law.

3. I understand the Servicer will pull a current credit report on all borrowers obligated on the Note.

4. I understand that if I have intentionally defaulted on my existing mortgage, engaged in fraud or misrepresented any fact(s) in connection with this document, the Servicer may cancel any Agreement under Making Home Affordable and may pursue foreclosure on my home.

5. That: my property is owner-occupied; I intend to reside in this property for the next twelve months; I have not received a condemnation notice; and there has been no change in the ownership of the Property since I signed the documents for the mortgage that I want to modify.

6. I am willing to provide all requested documents and to respond to all Servicer questions in a timely manner.

7. I understand that the Servicer will use the information in this document to evaluate my eligibility for a loan modification or short sale or deed-in-lieu of foreclosure, but the Servicer is not obligated to offer me assistance based solely on the statements in this document.

8. I am willing to commit to credit counseling if it is determined that my financial hardship is related to excessive debt.

9. I understand that the Servicer will collect and record personal information, including, but not limited to, my name, address, telephone number, social security number, credit score, income, payment history, government monitoring information, and information about account balances and activity. I understand and consent to the disclosure of my personal information and the terms of any Making Home Affordable Agreement by Servicer to (a) the U.S. Department of the Treasury, (b) Fannie Mae and Freddie Mac in connection with their responsibilities under the Homeowner Affordability and Stability Plan; (c) any investor, insurer, guarantor or servicer that owns, insures, guarantees or services my first lien or subordinate lien (if applicable) mortgage loan(s); (d) companies that perform support services in conjunction with Making Home Affordable; and (e) any HUD-certified housing counselor.

▷ _____   _____

Borrower Signature   Date

▷ _____   _____

Co-Borrower Signature   Date

HOMEOWNER'S HOTLINE

If you have questions about this document or the modification process, please call your servicer.

If you have questions about the program that your servicer cannot answer or need further counseling, you can call the Homeowner's HOPE™ Hotline at 1-888-995-HOPE (4673). The Hotline can help with questions about the program and offers free HUD-certified counseling services in English and Spanish.

888-995-HOPE
Homeowner's HOPE™ Hotline

NOTICE TO BORROWERS

Be advised that by signing this document you understand that any documents and information you submit to your servicer in connection with the Making Home Affordable Program are under penalty of perjury. Any misstatement of material fact made in the completion of these documents including but not limited to misstatement regarding your occupancy in your home, hardship circumstances, and/or income, expenses, or assets will subject you to potential criminal investigation and prosecution for the following crimes: perjury, false statements, mail fraud, and wire fraud. The information contained in these documents is subject to examination and verification. Any potential misrepresentation will be referred to the appropriate law enforcement authority for investigation and prosecution. By signing this document you certify, represent and agree that "Under penalty of perjury, all documents and information I have provided to Lender in connection with the Making Home Affordable Program, including the documents and information regarding my eligibility for the program, are true and correct."

If you are aware of fraud, waste, abuse, mismanagement or misrepresentations affiliated with the Troubled Asset Relief Program, please contact the SIGTARP Hotline by calling 1-877-SIG-2009 (toll-free), 202-622-4559 (fax), or www.sigtarp.gov. Mail can be sent to Hotline Office of the Special Inspector General for Troubled Asset Relief Program, 1801 L St. NW, Washington, DC 20220.

page 3 of 3

www.ingramcontent.com/pod-product-compliance
Lightning Source LLC
Chambersburg PA
CBHW051352200326
41521CB00014B/2546